What Is in the Wind?

by Erik Barneveld

HOUGHTON MIFFLIN HARCOURT
School Publishers

ILLUSTRATION CREDIT: Dan Trush

PHOTOGRAPHY CREDITS: Cover HMCo./Getty Images. 1 Photodisc/Alamy. 2-3 HMCo./Getty Images. 4-5 Peter Evans/Alamy. 6-7 Joe Sohm/VisionsofAmerica/Getty Images. 7 (inset) Don Farrall/PhotoDisc/Getty Images. 8-9 National Geographic/Getty Images. 9 (inset) © Rudi Von Briel/PhotoEdit . (inset) © David Young-Wolff/PhotoEdit. 10 © SuperStock.

Printed in India

ISBN-13: 978-0-547-02296-3
ISBN-10: 0-547-02296-4

2 3 4 5 6 7 8 0940 18 17 16 15 14 13 12 11 10

Sensing the Wind

You can feel the wind blow. Your hair blows in the breeze. You can also see the wind blow. The wind can bend branches. It can send a kite sailing through the sky.

Moving Wind

Wind is moving air. When the sun warms the ground, air near the ground gets warmer. The warm air is lighter and moves up. Cooler air moves down and fills in the place where the warm air was. This movement of air makes wind.

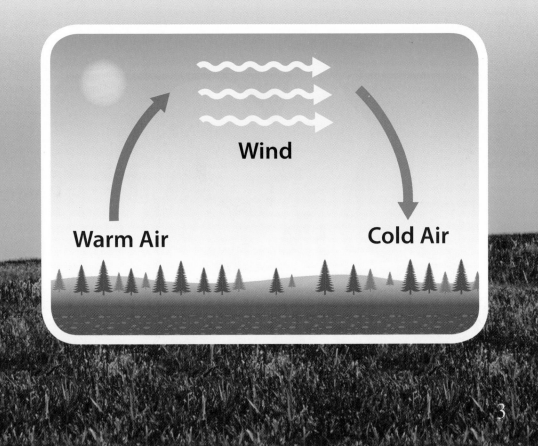

Measuring Wind

Wind is measured by the direction it comes from. A weather vane is often found on top of a building or barn. Its arrow moves to show the direction the wind is coming from. Wind is also measured by its speed. A breeze moves at a slow speed and is very gentle. The wind in storms moves at a fast speed and is very strong.

Helpful Winds

Wind can be useful to people! On hot days, wind helps people stay cool. The wind also helps sailboats move over the water. Windmills use the wind to grind wheat and corn to make flour and other kinds of food.

Wind can also make electricity. Wind towers stand in places called "wind farms." The wind turns the arms on towers, and the turning arms make electricity. Wind farms need a lot of wind. The amount of wind is not equal in all places. There is usually more wind on hills and near oceans. Wind farms are often built near these places.

Harmful Winds

Not all winds are useful to people. Strong winds can do a lot of damage. They can hurt people, trees, and buildings. A tornado is a powerful storm. Its winds can reach the speed of fast trains. Tornado winds can tear trees out of the ground and destroy buildings.

Hurricanes are powerful storms that begin over the ocean. Lightning flashes usually are not seen in hurricanes. But hurricanes can make very strong winds. The winds blow the ocean water and make big waves. When hurricanes get near the shore, these big, pounding waves are dangerous.

People watch storm warnings on the television and listen on the radio. Storm warnings tell people to beware of the storm. They tell people to protect themselves. When there is a storm warning, people try to prevent damage from wind and water. They try to make their homes safe. Many leave their homes and go to a safe place.

After a storm is gone, the wind is no longer dangerous and becomes helpful again. On most days, the wind is a useful friend that helps us work and have fun!

Responding

What details did you learn about the wind?
Copy and complete the web below.

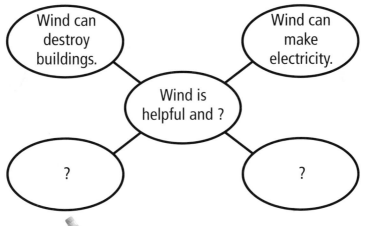

Wind can destroy buildings.

Wind can make electricity.

Wind is helpful and ?

?

?

✏ Write About It

Text to Text What other books have you read about the weather? Write a few sentences that summarize one of those books. Remember that summarizing means telling the most important ideas in a few sentences.

bend	flash
beware	pounding
damage	prevent
equal	reach

✔ **TARGET SKILL** **Main Ideas and Details**
Tell important ideas and details about a topic.

✔ **TARGET STRATEGY** **Visualize** Picture what is happening as you read.

GENRE **Informational text** gives facts about a topic.